B

TRAILER

The Complete And Practical Guide
On How To Build Teardrop Trailer

Dr Jack Kelly

Table of Contents

CHAPTER ONE 3

    INTRODUCTION TO HOW TO BUILD A TEAR DROP CAMBER 3

CHAPTER TWO 7

    WHAT YOU NEE TO KNOW ABOUT GTEAR DROP CAMPER 7

CHAPTER THREE...10

    THE RESURGENECE OF TEARDROP CAMPER 10

CHAPTER FOUR 13

    HOW TO BUILD A TEAR DROP CAMBER 13

CHAPTER FIVE 18

    WHAT YOU NEED TO KNOW ABOUT MOTORCYCLE TEARDROP CAMPERS............18

CHAPTER SIX 21

    TEAR DROP AND ITS TECHNIQUES 21

THE END 23

CHAPTER ONE

INTRODUCTION TO HOW TO BUILD A TEAR DROP CAMBER

tear drop trailer–few mobile sleeping accommodations are as personal as this one. With a limited amount of space, the person who builds and uses one has to make tough decisions regarding what to include and what to omit.

In a nutshell, this is how to build a teardrop trailer:

The foundation – you'll need a frame to use for the wheels, lights, and rest of the trailer to sit on

The sides – install walls using wooden frames, add exhaust fan, metal roof, doors, windows, and fenders

The Galley and interior – install wiring, insulation, cabinets, and shelves

The Finish – use a dye for the base exterior color, add a few layers of epoxy to the finish

Enjoy your custom teardrop trailer

The basic design of a Teardrop trailer includes an interior sleeping space and a galley kitchen accessible from the back. These small trailers are aerodynamic and light-weight, and can be easily pulled with a car, making them ecologically and economically friendly. They are also relatively easy to build for a minimal investment.

Handy man and Teardrop enthusiast, Ryan decided to build his very own trailer. The entire process took about seven months to complete. He documented the build Take a look at the process he went through to turn his plans into reality. Who knows, maybe you will be inspired to build your own teardrop! Teardrop Trailer Builds to Inspire Your Haulable Home

Teardrop campers are absolutely wonderful. They're the tiniest of the trailers, sometimes even having a smaller footprint than a tent, but with all the amenities of a home. They are extremely popular not only because they can be relatively cheap, but they're also fairly easy to build.

Before you set off on your journey to build the ultimate teardrop trailer, you'll need some inspiration. Here are 11 trailer builds to give you ideas and tips for your build.

CHAPTER TWO

WHAT YOU NEE TO KNOW ABOUT GTEAR DROP CAMPER

Teardrop Campers

A teardrop camper is a light weight mini camper in the shape of a teardrop. There is one basic design for a teardrop. Builders will modify the teardrop to fit their own personal dream. A bed is all that is in the main area. On the back there is a hatch door with a galley area. Some teardrops have kitchens and others just use the back galley as storage.

History of Teardrop Campers

Teardrop camper designs became popular once world war 2 ended. Families wanted to travel and take vacations but wanted small lightweight travel trailers. There was such a surplus of supplies around it was easy to make a teardrop out of left over supplies. Small Jeep trailers and parts were often used along with plane parts.

You could even find published teardrop trailer plans in magazines like Popular Mechanics.

Teardrop trailers were all the rage in the late 40's. Because the cars were only about 100 horsepower at that time the trailers needed to be light enough to tow. There were even teardrop trailers designed for motorcycles. Around the start of the 50's the teardrop craze started dying down. Cars with more horsepower were being built in true American fashion. So the size of campers grew along with the cars.

CHAPTER THREE

THE RESURGENECE OF TEARDROP CAMPER

Resurgence of Teardrop Campers

The past few years has seen a renewed interest in teardrop trailers. Building and traveling in a teardrop camper has a cult like following. As this community grows the teardrop camper has seen a comeback. In the united states they are mostly called teardrop trailers or just teardrops. They have become popular in Australia too where they call them teardrop campers.

Teardrop campers are light and smaller vehicles can tow them. This makes them an attractive inexpensive camping option. Check the specs on your car to stay under the towing limit. It's a good idea to call the manufacture and talk with them. The information in a car manual can be deceiving. The way they calculate towing limits are are not always accurate. You will find stories of blown engines and major mechanical issues all over the forums. Be smart and stay under the weight limit.

Buy or Build a Teardrop Camper

If you are reading this I'm sure you have a slight interest in teardrops and have caught the bug. There are two options for those looking for a Teardrop Camper. You can buy one new or used OR you can build your own.

CHAPTER FOUR

HOW TO BUILD A TEAR DROP CAMBER

It takes a special kind of person to build a teardrop. You need to commit to the project and be a good problem solver. Building a teardrop is not for everyone. I know the idea of building one sounds awesome but don't kid yourself, it will be a challenge. In saying all that I still don't want to discourage anyone if they really want to build a teardrop.

There are a ton of useful resources and friendly people on line. Check out the TNTTT (Teardrops N Tiny Travel Trailers) forum. They will help you work through any problems you come across. So if it's something you want to do, I say go for it! You only have one life, you might as well try.

Teardrop Camper

Not everyone is handy and cut out to build things. Buying a Teardrop

Camper would be the best option for you. There are some great Teardrop builders out there. Make sure you do your homework. Talk to others who have purchased their teardrops and see how their experience was. Some of the builders with a great reputation can have a long wait list. I've seen a wait list of up to 2 years for a custom built teardrop camper.

Here are a couple examples of Teardrop builders.

Timberleaf Trailers

Vestibule

I have no experience with these companies. I do not know if they are good or bad, I picked a few from a quick Google search.

Buy a Used Teardrop Camper

Another option is to buy a used teardrop. This can be a tricky process. There are different laws in each state regarding home built trailers. Do your due diligence in this area. Make sure you have all the info you need. Registration, titles, insurance, and regulations vary from state to state. Know all the laws BEFORE you buy a teardrop. Buying a commercially made trailer is not as much of an issue as buying a homebuilt teardrop.

Commercial builders have to follow federal standards when they build a teardrop. This will give you some peace of mind when buying a used trailer. Buying a commercially built trailer can also be much more expensive. A used home built or building your own teardrop can be cheaper.

Like anything in life there are different sub segments of teardrop campers. Some people like being able to take a quick weekend getaway. Jump in the car and have a nice relaxing time without much planning.

CHAPTER FIVE

WHAT YOU NEED TO KNOW ABOUT MOTORCYCLE TEARDROP CAMPERS

There's even a group of motorcycle teardrop campers.

Sometimes these groups overlap but one thing is clear, they LOVE their teardrops. Throughout the country there are teardrop meet ups. If you would like to find one near you check the forums. Picture a car meet up you would see in a dinner parking lot, only these are for a few days and with teardrops. If you are a people person they are a lot of fun.

Off Road Teardrop Campers

There's a group of off road campers in Canada called 410 Expedition. You can find them on and they are pretty much crazy people. They will go up in the mountains in Canada and go camp in the wilderness. They have a whole team of people with beefed up trucks and trailers. It's very entertaining following them.

They have a guy in their group called Cappy. He has a few videos on their channel about building an off road teardrop camper. It's worth watching. You can learn a lot about camping off road in a teardrop camper.

Teardrop Camper Roadtrip

Each style of camping in a

CHAPTER SIX

TEAR DROP AND ITS TECHNIQUES

teardrop has its own unique set of challenges. Going on a long road trip is no exception. This category could have a few sub categories of its own. There are short term road trips all the way up to those who only live in their teardrop. Almost off grid minimalists.

To take your teardrop on any sort of road trip you need to prepare. Prepare like your life depends on it. You need to have great backup plan in place or be great at fixing things. If you have both of those it would be even better.

Talk to teardroppers who have gone on the type of road trip you are thinking about. They will be a wealth of information and show you things you would never have thought of on your own.

THE END

Made in the USA
Middletown, DE
14 October 2021